W9-BSL-309

Valparaiso Public Library
103 Jefferson St.
Valparaiso, IN 46383

LAUNCH DAY

LAUNCH DAY

Written and illustrated
by Peter A. Campbell

PORTER COUNTY PUBLIC LIBRARY SYSTEM

Valparaiso Public Library
103 Jefferson St.
Valparaiso, IN 46383

The Millbrook Press
Brookfield, Connecticut

DEC 2 2 1997

J 629.45 CAM   VAL
Campbell, Peter A.
Launch day /
33410004404986

The workers at the John F. Kennedy Space Center, located in the state of Florida, are very happy this morning. The weather is beautiful, and all signs are "go" for the launch of the Space Shuttle *Atlantis*.

The Kennedy Space Center is a very special place. From launch pads close to the center's flat, sandy beaches on the Atlantic Ocean, giant Saturn V rockets were launched into space in the 1960s and 1970s. These powerful rockets carried astronauts to the moon.

Today, if everything goes well, the shuttle *Atlantis* will blast off into space. The shuttle is America's first real spaceship. It blasts off like a rocket and lands like an airplane. Preparing the *Atlantis* for a mission requires a lot of hard work and preparation.

Months before a launch, the *Atlantis*'s orbiter is given a full overhaul at the Orbiter Processing Facility at the Kennedy Space Center. NASA(National Aeronautics and Space Administration) workers inspect over 24,000 specially-designed silica tiles that cover much of the *Atlantis*.

These lightweight tiles form a heat shield around the aluminum structure of the orbiter that protects the astronauts in space. A reinforced carbon-carbon material is used to protect the orbiter's nose, wing tips and vertical stabilizer. This is important, because temperatures can reach 3,000° F (1,649° C) as the shuttle *Atlantis* re-enters the Earth's atmosphere from space. Once this work is completed, the *Atlantis* can be towed to the Vehicle Assembly Building nearby.

The Vehicle Assembly Building is enormous! It stands over 525 feet (160 meters) high and covers 8 acres (3.2 hectares) of land. The powerful Saturn V rockets that took Neil Armstrong, Buzz Aldrin, and Michael Collins to the Moon in July 1969 were assembled upright in this building. In time for the 1981 launch of America's first space shuttle, *Columbia*, the Vehicle Assembly Building was modified to handle this whole new generation of spacecraft. Oh, one more thing! See that American flag painted on the outside of the Vehicle Assembly Building? It measures 110 feet (33 meters) wide by 209 feet (63 meters) long! 6,000 gallons (22,800 liters) of paint were needed in order to create America's national symbol.

Once inside the Vehicle Assembly Building, the shuttle is placed into a support sling. It is then lifted high into the air by a powerful bridge crane. Guided by two highly-skilled operators, the *Atlantis* is carefully lowered onto the mobile launch platform below. Once in place, the shuttle is attached to the external fuel tank. When the spaceship is assembled it stands over 185 feet (55 meters) high. It is an incredible sight!

The shuttle is now ready to begin its 3.5 mile (5.5 kilometer) journey to Launch Pad B. Slowly, the massive bay doors of the Vehicle Assembly Building are opened, revealing a beautiful star-filled sky.

The solid rocket boosters are assembled on the mobile launch platform.

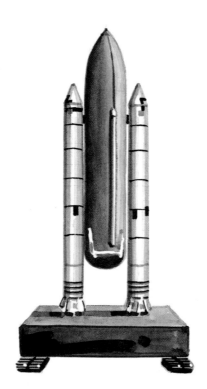

Next, the external fuel tank is attached to the solid rocket boosters.

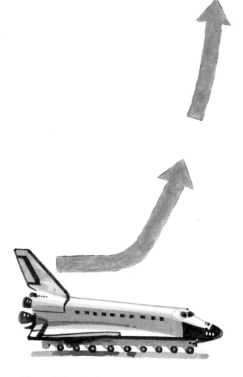

The orbiter is brought into the Vehicle Assembly Building on a flatbed vehicle.

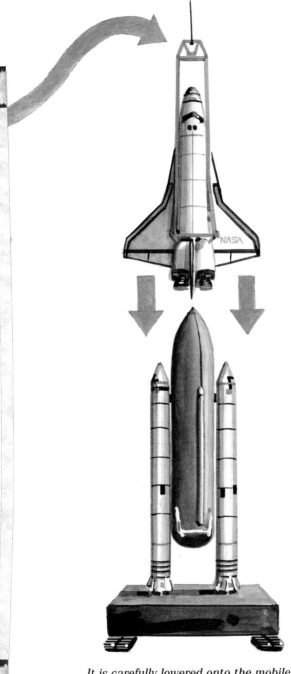

It is carefully lowered onto the mobile launch platform and attached to the external fuel tank.

The Tractor-Transporter Vehicle, on which the shuttle sits, is the largest transport vehicle in the world. It has been nicknamed the "crawler" by NASA engineers, because it travels 1 mile (1.6 kilometers) per hour with the shuttle as its cargo. Why so slow? Because the combined weight of the shuttle, mobile launch platform, and "crawler" totals 7,600 tons!

Two operators, sitting in enclosed glass cabs at each end of the transporter, do the driving. Even though the transporter moves at a snail's pace, the operators must wear seatbelts. If you stare at the "crawler" long enough, it begins to look like a mechanical bug-eyed creature from outer space.

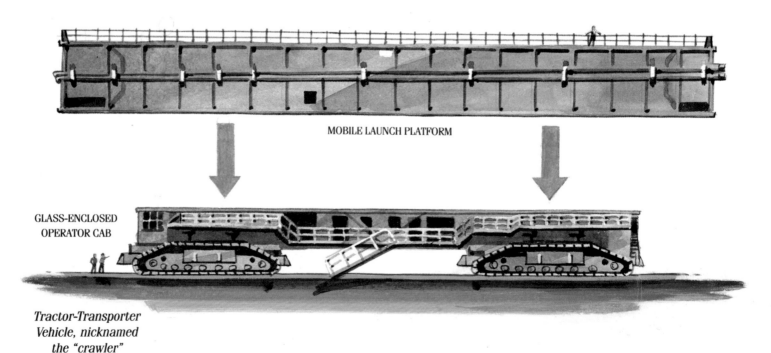

MOBILE LAUNCH PLATFORM

GLASS-ENCLOSED
OPERATOR CAB

*Tractor-Transporter
Vehicle, nicknamed
the "crawler"*

The "crawler" moves on eight giant steel tracks. Each track contains 57 cleats. Each cleat weighs one ton!

The transporter is traveling to Launch Pad B on a special road called the Crawlerway. With a surface composed of river rocks, the Crawlerway is 8 feet (244 centimeters) thick at the turns and 4 inches (10 centimeters) thick over straightaways. It is designed to support the tremendous weight of the "crawler" and shuttle.

As the *Atlantis* completes its four-hour journey, a docking system helps park the shuttle in a special spot next to two giant service towers. The larger of the two stands over 340 feet (103 meters) high. It is connected to the shuttle and will provide an entrance for service crews and astronauts. The smaller tower is mounted on a curved track and can swing away from the shuttle's orbiter. It is used to load heavy items, such as large satellites and space telescopes, into the shuttle's cargo bay.

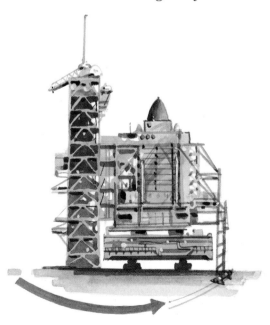

View of service towers as they appear when a payload is being placed into the shuttle cargo bay.

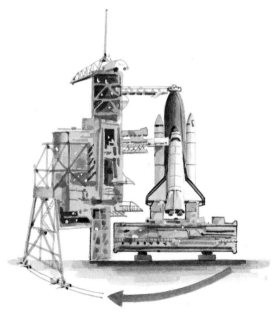

Hours before the launch, the smaller service tower is rolled back, freeing the shuttle for takeoff.

Just as the engineers and vehicle operators have prepared the *Atlantis* for its flight into space, the astronauts of the *Atlantis* have prepared for the journey. For over a year, they have been training for their mission at the Johnson Space Center in Houston, Texas, where all astronauts are trained. Today, at the operation and checkout facilities—only a few miles from the launch area—the astronauts are kept in quarantine. It is very important to protect the astronauts from catching a cold or the flu.

Today the astronauts begin their morning with a light breakfast. Afterward, they proceed to a special room in the Operations and Checkout Building, where they suit up for the launch. The launch and entry suits are flame resistant and can be pressurized during an emergency. The suits are orange in color. The helmet must be worn during the launch and when the shuttle re-enters Earth's atmosphere at the end of the mission.

As the astronauts suit up, they are briefed and updated on the most current launch conditions. Soon the astronauts will be given the signal to proceed to the launch area.

While waiting, some of the astronauts review their flight plans. Others sit quietly thinking of their families. But all crew members are quite aware of the danger that surrounds a space shuttle launch. The shuttle *Challenger* exploded only 78 seconds into its flight on January 28, 1986. Today, the memory of the *Challenger* crew lives on in the hearts and minds of these new space pioneers.

The moment the astronauts have all been waiting for has arrived. Led by their commander, the astronauts leave the Operations and Checkout Building. All NASA technicians and well-wishers cheer and applaud. The astronauts board a shiny aluminum shuttle bus. The drive to Launch Pad B will take about ten minutes.

One of the best spots for viewing a shuttle launch is the press area. It is located 3.5 miles (5.6 kilometers) inland from Launch Pad B. This morning, over a thousand people have crowded into the press area. Reporters, photographers, scientists, and NASA artists are all busy preparing for the final countdown.

Just across the river, the shuttle bus has arrived at Launch Pad B. TV monitors, located throughout the grandstand area, give visitors a close-up view of the astronauts as they enter the shuttle's orbiter through a circular hatch measuring 40 inches (100 centimeters) in diameter.

Inside the crew compartment, NASA technicians help the astronauts strap themselves in for the final countdown.

With only ten minutes left in the countdown, excitement begins to build all around the Cape and also at the Johnson Space Center in Houston, Texas.

When the *Atlantis* leaves the launch pad this morning, ground controllers in Houston will take charge of the shuttle. They will monitor the shuttle and its crew's activities until its scheduled landing at the Kennedy Space Center a few days from now. The ground controllers will accomplish this by using rows of computer and communications consoles. The shuttle will send back live TV images that appear on large TV screens in the mission control room. A large electronic map of the world will show the exact location of the shuttle while in orbit.

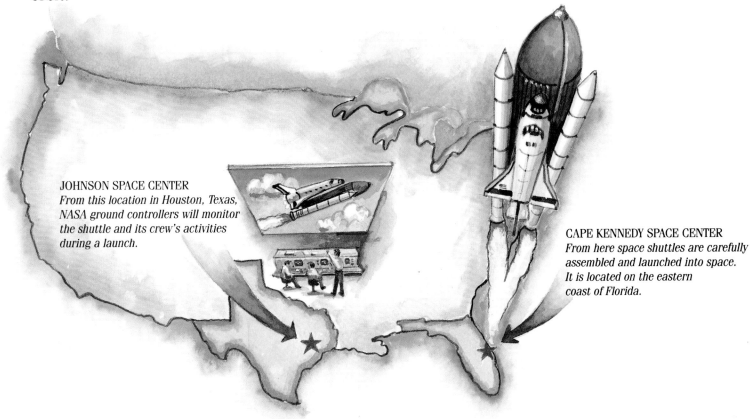

JOHNSON SPACE CENTER
From this location in Houston, Texas, NASA ground controllers will monitor the shuttle and its crew's activities during a launch.

CAPE KENNEDY SPACE CENTER
From here space shuttles are carefully assembled and launched into space. It is located on the eastern coast of Florida.

Back at the Kennedy Space Center, the anxious astronauts are strapped into their seats. The flight director is in contact with the crew to review the final flight instructions with them. The external fuel tank has been filled with a half million pounds (225,000 kilograms) of liquid hydrogen and oxygen. With seven minutes left in the countdown, the access arm is detached from the shuttle.

Two minutes left and all systems are still "go". At T (take-off) minus 31 seconds, the computers on board the *Atlantis* take control. The astronauts begin to feel the shuttle come alive as the three main engines move into their final launch position.

The giant digital clock at the press area shows only seconds until blast off.

With six seconds left in the countdown, the liquid hydrogen and oxygen begin to travel down separate hoses to the three main engines below. They ignite to produce more than 1.18 million pounds (535,000 kilograms) of thrust. At T minus 0, the two solid fuel rocket boosters ignite, adding another 5.8 million pounds (2.7 million kilograms) of thrust.

We have lift-off!

HOUR   MINUTE   SECOND

Slowly, the *Atlantis* begins to rise. Enormous clouds of smoke and steam billow up all around the launch pad. As the *Atlantis* lifts off, three hundred thousand gallons (1.1 million liters) of water begin to pour over the mobile launch pad and into the concrete flame trenches below. This will help absorb some of the tremendous sound and shaking generated by the three main engines. It is important to protect the shuttle's fragile wings and its valuable payload from this vibration.

Now, the blinding yellow-orange flame of the powerful rocket is visible just above the mountains of smoke and exhaust. Suddenly, the earth begins to rumble.

Birds of every type take to the air around the launch area. Brown pelicans, terns, the great blue heron, and the wood stork are startled from their nests by the launch of the giant mechanical bird, *Atlantis*. It is truly a celebration of flight.

Back at the press area, all eyes are riveted on this magnificent spaceship born of dreams, metal, and fire. For the first few moments, from this location, the shuttle appears to rise in silence. Suddenly a faint crackling sound is heard. It grows louder and louder every second. Some of the viewers cover their ears with their hands to block out the deafening sound. Others applaud and cheer the *Atlantis* onward as it struggles to break free of Earth's gravitational pull.

It is a bumpy ride for the astronauts. Two minutes into the flight, the astronauts feel the two solid rocket boosters break away from the external fuel tank, making the ride much smoother. The solid rocket boosters will fall to Earth by parachute. They will be recovered later from the Atlantic Ocean, and used for a future flight.

As the shuttle reaches an altitude of about 100 miles (160 kilometers), it is traveling close to 17,000 miles (27,000 kilometers) per hour. The astronauts shut off the main engines and release the empty external fuel tank. The tank will break up and fall into the Indian Ocean. About nine minutes have passed since the *Atlantis* left its fiery launch pad at the Cape Kennedy Space Center in Florida. The shuttle, now a true spaceship free of fuel tanks, orbits about 200 miles (320 kilometers) above blue-green Earth. What a beautiful sight!

The astronauts are now weightless and can move around the flight deck with little effort.

Once in orbit the astronauts are eager to get to work. Depending on the mission, they may perform scientific experiments dealing with the long-term effects of weightlessness. They may photograph Earth from space to help study the effect of air pollution on Earth's environment. Astronauts are not the only life forms from Earth that have flown aboard the space shuttle. Flies, tadpoles, hornets, and even rats have been closely observed and monitored on special laboratory research missions.

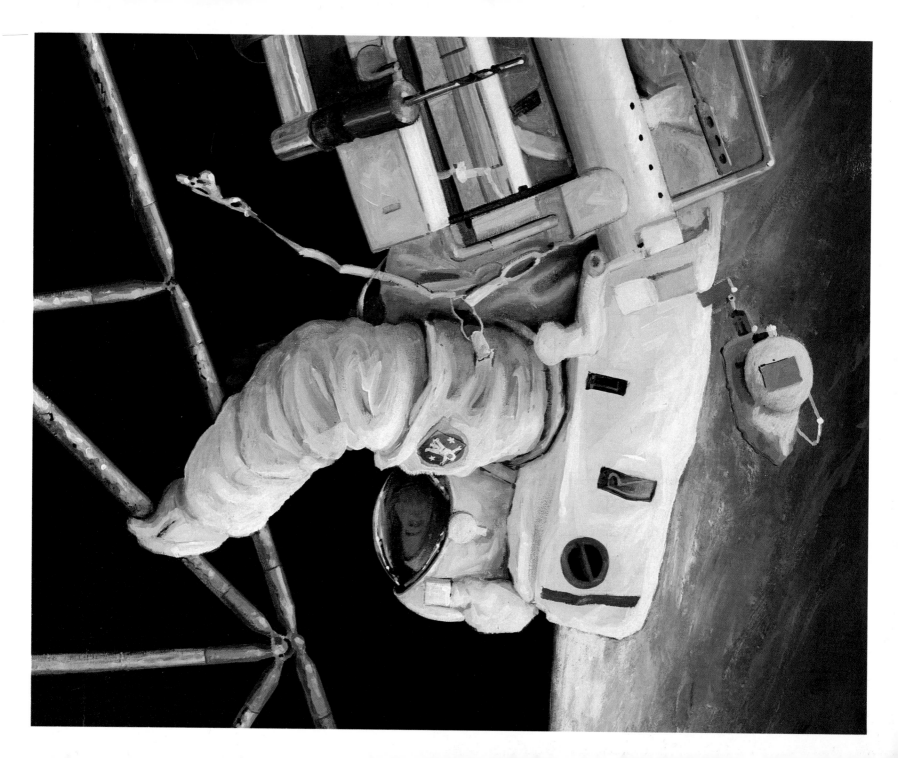

During certain flights astronauts have to leave their comfortable earthly environment aboard the shuttle to repair or retrieve satellites, telescopes, or other space apparatus. For this work spacesuits and helmets must be worn. If the astronauts are required to float away from the shuttle, a small rocketpack is worn. It has little gas jets that allow the astronaut to maneuver in any direction.

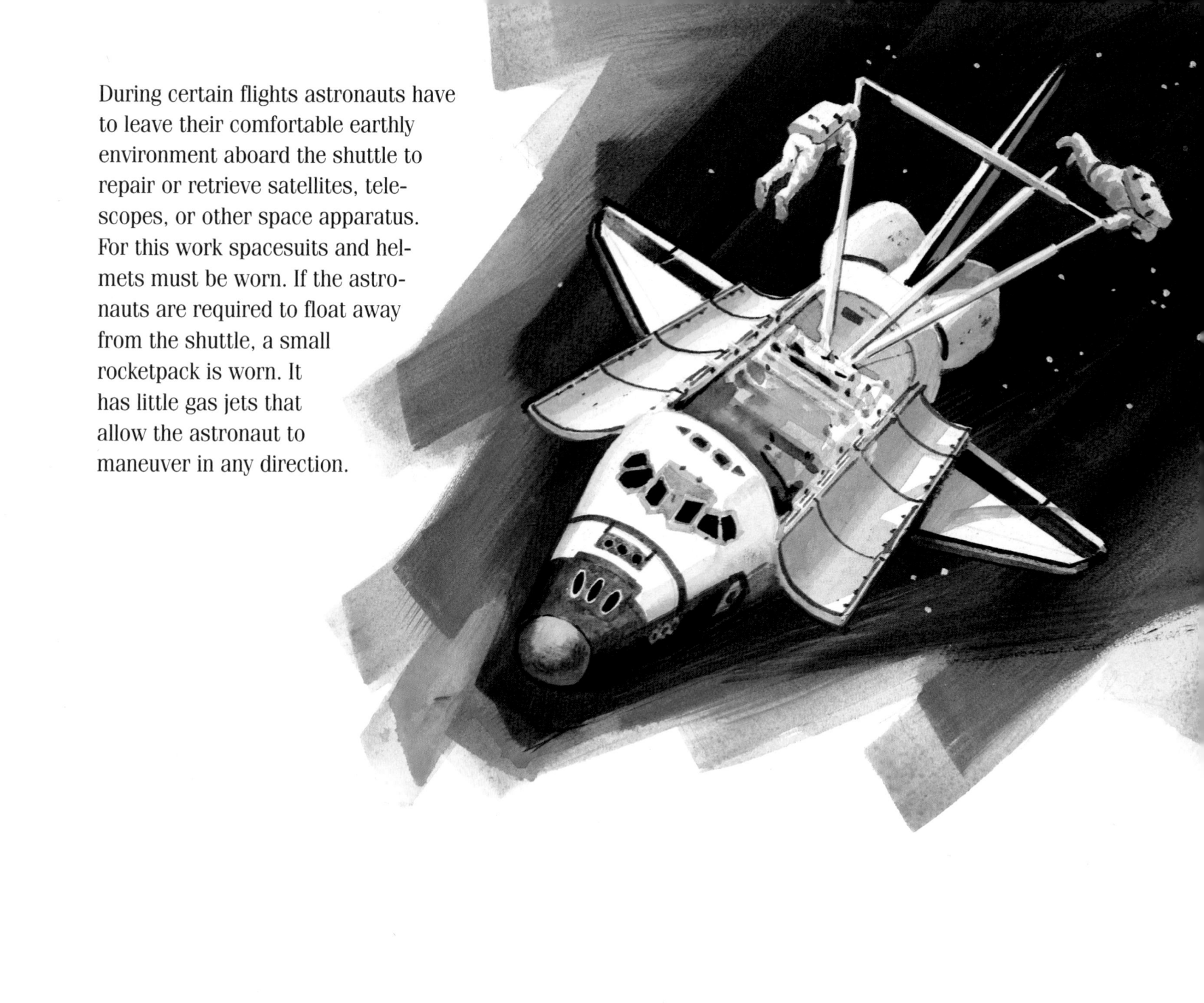

At the end of their mission, after days in orbit, the astronauts will begin to prepare for their journey home. The shuttle's sophisticated guidance system, together with the help of the controllers at the Johnson Space Center, will bring the orbiter back to Earth.

The commander fires the engines located near the shuttle's tail. This slows down the orbiter and allows it to re-enter Earth's atmosphere. For the next fifteen minutes, the *Atlantis* is subjected to tremendous heat.

A large crowd has gathered at the Kennedy Space Center.

After a short wait, the shuttle, looking like a small silver speck against the bright blue sky, is spotted by the enthusiastic crowd.

The pilot of the shuttle knows the landing must be perfect. There is no fuel left for a second attempt. As the *Atlantis* touches down on the runway, it is traveling at about 200 miles (320 kilometers) per hour. The wheel brakes are applied and a 40-foot-wide (12 meters) drag parachute is opened to slow the shuttle. Finally, the gleaming white bird comes to a stop near the end of the 3-mile-long (4.8-kilometer) runway.

A platform with stairs is rolled up to the shuttle, and the proud crew emerges, waving to the cheering crowd. Mission accomplished!

For Karen, Seth, Jeremy, and Brendan

Special thanks to Robert Schulman and the wonderful people at NASA. And to Ray Bradbury, who showed me the magic and power of the rocket.

And to my special friends Kathy Silvestry and Thom Valentino, who helped make this book a reality.

Library of Congress Cataloging-in-Publication data
Campbell, Peter A.
Launch Day/written and illustrated by Peter A. Campbell.
p. cm
Summary: Describes preparation, launch, and return of the Atlantis space shuttle at Cape Kennedy Space Center in Florida.
ISBN 1-56294-611-0 (lib. bdg.). ISBN 1-56294-190-9 (pbk.)
1. John F. Kennedy Space Center—Juvenile literature. 2. Atlantis (Space Shuttle)—Juvenile literature. [1. John F Kennedy Space Center. 2. Atlantis (Space Shuttle) 3. Space shuttles.]
I. Title.
TL4027.F52J636 1995
629.454'00973—dc20   95-22820   CIP AC

Published by The Millbrook Press
2 Old New Milford Road
Brookfield, Connecticut 06804

Copyright © 1995 by Peter A. Campbell
All rights reserved
Printed in the United States of America